TOP TRUMPS®

STAR WARS™

No part of this publication may be reproduced or transmitted in any form or by
any means, electronic or mechanical, including photocopying, recording or by
any information storage or retrieval system, without permission in writing from
Haynes Publishing.

This book is officially licensed by Winning Moves UK Ltd,
owners of the Top Trumps registered trademark.

Benjamin Harper has asserted his right
to be identified as the author of this book.

First published in November 2008

British Library Cataloguing-in-Publication Data:
A catalogue record for this book is available from the British Library

ISBN 978 1 84425 654 9

Library of Congress catalog card no. 2008929395

Published by Haynes Publishing,
Sparkford, Yeovil, Somerset BA22 7JJ, UK
Tel: 01963 442030 Fax: 01963 440001
Int. tel: +44 1963 442030 Int. fax: +44 1963 440001
Email: sales@haynes.co.uk
Website: www.haynes.co.uk

Haynes North America, Inc.,
861 Lawrence Drive, Newbury Park, California 91320, USA

Designed by Lee Parsons

Printed and bound in Great Britain by J. H. Haynes & Co. Ltd, Sparkford

The Author

Benjamin Harper is an editor at DC Comics and author. He has written several
Star Wars titles, including *Obsessed With Star Wars* and *Star Wars Revenge of
the Sith Trivia Quest*. He currently lives in New York City.

TOP TRUMPS

STAR WARS

CONTENTS

It's now more than 30 years since Britain's kids first caught the Top Trumps craze. The game remained hugely popular until the 1990s, when it slowly drifted into obscurity. Then, in 1999, UK games company Winning Moves discovered it, bought it, dusted it down, gave it a thorough makeover and introduced it to a whole new generation. And so the Top Trumps legend continues.

Nowadays, there are Top Trumps titles for just about everyone, with subjects about animals, cars, ships, aircraft and all the great films and TV shows. Top Trumps is now even more popular than before. In Britain, a pack of Top Trumps is bought every six seconds! And it's not just British children who love the game. Children in Australasia, the Far East, the Middle East, all over Europe and in North America can buy Top Trumps at their local shops.

Today you can even play the game on the internet, interactive DVD, your games console and even your mobile phone.

YOU'VE PLAYED THE GAME...

NOW READ THE BOOK

Haynes Publishing and Top Trumps have teamed up to bring you
this exciting new Top Trumps book, in which you will find even more
pictures, details and statistics.

Top Trumps: Star Wars features 45 characters from *Star Wars*:
Episodes IV, V and VI – from the young Luke Skywalker and Jedi
Master Obi-Wan Kenobi to the corrupt Jabba the Hutt, the evil Darth
Vader and his Master Emperor Palpatine. Packed with fascinating
facts, stunning film stills and all the vital statistics, this is the essential
pocket guide.

Look out for other Top Trumps books from Haynes Publishing
– even more facts, even more fun!

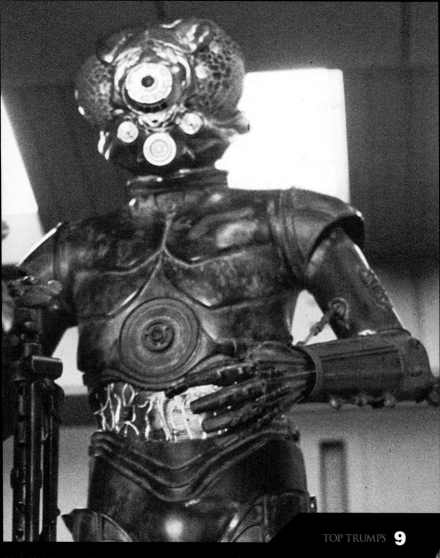

4-LOM

4-LOM began its career as an average, unthinking protocol droid aboard the starship *Kuari Princess*, catering to passengers' needs. Over time, 4-LOM grew restless and began engaging the ship's computer in conversation, and decided to steal a rare gem from a careless guest. After this, 4-LOM found a new career as a thief – passengers never suspected the protocol droid would think to do such a thing. Jabba the Hutt, impressed by the former protocol droid's initiative, gave it a programming upgrade and turned it into one of the most sought-after bounty hunters in the galaxy. Jabba suggested that 4-LOM partner with another infamous hunter, the Gand findsman Zuckuss, and together the two gained a galactic reputation for hunting excellence.

4-LOM, along with Zuckuss, was called to the Super Star Destroyer *Executor* when Darth Vader issued a bounty for the capture of Han Solo and all passengers aboard the *Millennium Falcon*.

STATISTICS

DROID:	Industrial Automaton LOM-series protocol unit
HOMEWORLD:	Unknown
HEIGHT:	1.6m
STRENGTH:	**5**
INTELLIGENCE:	**7**
SPECIAL ABILITIES:	None
WEAPONRY:	**7** Concussion rifle, blaster pistol, stun-gas blower
VEHICLE:	*Mist Hunter*
BATTLE SKILLS:	**6**
ALLEGIANCE:	Bounty Hunter / Criminal
ALLIES:	Jabba the Hutt, Zuckuss
ENEMIES:	Boba Fett

ADMIRAL ACKBAR

Admiral Ackbar hails from the watery planet Mon Calamari where, before the Empire invaded, he was a representative for Coral Depths City on the Mon Calamari Council. When the Empire overtook the planet, Ackbar was taken prisoner and given to Grand Moff Tarkin as a slave. Though hardworking, Ackbar kept his eyes open and learned many Imperial secrets. Ackbar eventually escaped and lent his services to the Rebel Alliance.

Admiral Ackbar was in command of the Alliance Fleet that attacked the second Death Star above Endor. From his massive Mon Calamari star cruiser, Ackbar directed the epic space battle that crippled the Imperial fleet and in part allowed General Lando Calrissian to penetrate the Death Star's defences and destroy the space station from within.

STATISTICS

SPECIES:	Mon Calamari
HOMEWORLD:	Mon Calamari
HEIGHT:	1.8m
STRENGTH:	**5**
INTELLIGENCE:	**9**
SPECIAL ABILITIES:	Unknown
WEAPONRY:	Unknown
VEHICLE:	Mon Calamari star cruiser *Home One*
BATTLE SKILLS:	**9** Leadership
ALLEGIANCE:	Rebel Alliance
ALLIES:	Mon Mothma, Lando Calrissian
ENEMIES:	Darth Vader, Emperor Palpatine

ADMIRAL FIRMUS PIETT

Firmus Piett was one of the few Imperial Officers from the Outer Rim of the galaxy who was able to climb the ranks and make name for himself. While an officer in the galaxy's "backwater," Piett impressed the Empire with a heavy list of "arrests and suppressions," making his sector the most secure in the region. Due to his efficiency, Piett was given the honor of working in the Imperial Death Squadron.

As the Empire sent probes to countless systems to locate the Rebel Alliance's secret base, Piett noticed a reading from the Hoth system and alerted his commanding officer. Ozzel, incredulous, said to ignore the reading, but Darth Vader knew better and ordered the fleet to the icy world. When Ozzel disappointed Vader with his inept tactics, Vader disposed of the Admiral, promoting Piett to the position. Piett served aboard the Super Star Destroyer *Executor* until the Battle of Endor when a runaway A-wing fighter crashed into the lumbering craft, sending it crashing into the second Death Star.

STATISTICS

SPECIES:	Human
HOMEWORLD:	Axxila
HEIGHT:	1.65m
STRENGTH:	**6**
INTELLIGENCE:	**7**
SPECIAL ABILITIES:	**7** Leadership, efficiency
WEAPONRY:	Unknown
VEHICLE:	Super Star Destroyer *Executor*
BATTLE SKILLS:	**7** Leadership
ALLEGIANCE:	The Empire
ALLIES:	Darth Vader, Admiral Ozzel
ENEMIES:	Rebel Alliance

ADMIRAL KENDAL OZZEL

Kendal Ozzel used his family's name to climb political and military ladders, eventually attaining the rank of captain. He was an instructor at the Imperial Academy on Coruscant at the time the Death Star was destroyed. An instant dearth in Imperial officers created several chances for advancement, and Ozzel lucked into a position commanding the Imperial Death Squadron.

Scouring the galaxy for signs of the new Rebel base, Ozzel initially ignored Captain Piett's alert that there were signs of life in the icy Hoth system. Darth Vader overrode Ozzel's orders to ignore the life signs and ordered the Imperial fleet to the Hoth system. There, Ozzel decided to surprise the Rebellion and jumped out of hyperspace in range of the Rebels' scanners. The Rebels, alerted to the failed surprise attack, activated a shield around their base. Darth Vader, tired of Ozzel's bungling, dispatched the officer and promoted Captain Piett to Admiral as an instant replacement.

STATISTICS

SPECIES:	Human
HOMEWORLD:	Carida
HEIGHT:	1.7m
STRENGTH:	**5**
INTELLIGENCE:	**6**
SPECIAL ABILITIES:	Unknown
WEAPONRY:	Unknown
VEHICLE:	Super Star Destroyer *Executor*
BATTLE SKILLS:	Unknown
ALLEGIANCE:	Empire
ALLIES:	Captain Piett, Darth Vader
ENEMIES:	Darth Vader, Rebel Alliance

BERU LARS

Born to one of the most intrepid moisture farming families of Tatooine, Beru Whitesun grew up near the notorious spaceport Mos Eisley. Her family had perfected moisture farming over three generations, and Beru had no aspirations for space travel or extravagance, having found contentment in the harsh isolation of the Tatooine desert.

She met her future husband, Owen Lars, on a trip to Anchorhead, another prominent spaceport on the desert planet. The two married and worked together on a moisture farm, raising their nephew, Luke Skywalker, and sheltering him from the true nature of his family tree. While Beru was protective of young Skywalker, she also felt it important for the boy to leave the farm one day and follow his dreams. Sadly, she would never see those dreams realized. The Empire traced the droids that had jettisoned themselves from *Tantive IV* to the Lars homestead and, when they didn't find what they were looking for, took vengeance on the defenceless farmers.

STATISTICS

SPECIES:	Human
HOMEWORLD:	Tatooine
HEIGHT:	1.65m
STRENGTH:	**5**
INTELLIGENCE:	**6**
SPECIAL ABILITIES:	Unknown
WEAPONRY:	None
VEHICLE:	V-35 landspeeder
BATTLE SKILLS:	Unknown
ALLEGIANCE:	Other / Neutral
ALLIES:	Luke Skywalker, Owen Lars
ENEMIES:	Tusken Raiders, stormtroopers

BIB FORTUNA

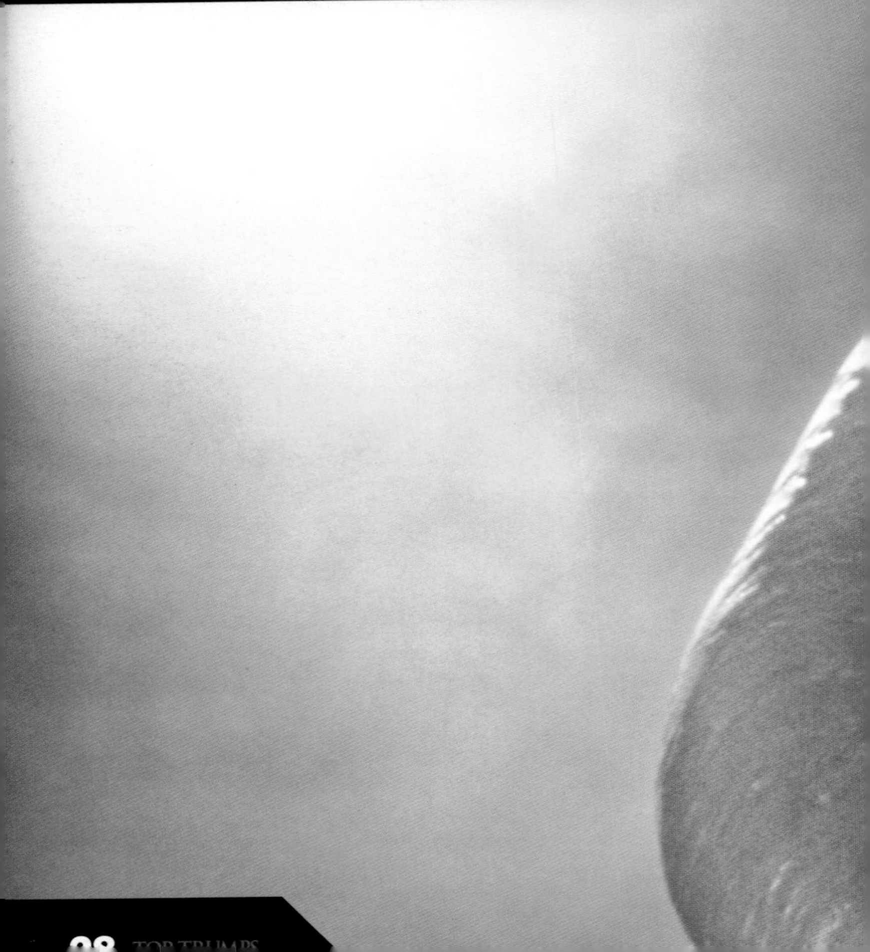

Born on the planet Ryloth in the Una clan, Bib Fortuna travelled off-world at a very young age and trafficked in spice. While his business was lucrative, it brought slavers to Ryloth. Fortuna was sentenced to death but escaped the planet, working his way into a position in Jabba's crime empire.

Fortuna worked for Jabba for forty years, eventually becoming the Hutt's confidante and major domo. Anyone attempting to gain an audience with Jabba the Hutt had first to get past his pasty, sharp-toothed Twi'lek. Fortuna did his job aggressively well until he fell victim to a Jedi mind trick when Luke Skywalker appeared at Jabba's palace. Despite orders from Jabba to the contrary, Bib Fortuna allowed Skywalker to gain entrance to the palace and set off a series of events that led to the crime lord's demise and the rescue of Han Solo.

STATISTICS

SPECIES:	Twi'lek
HOMEWORLD:	Ryloth
HEIGHT:	1.8m
STRENGTH:	**6**
INTELLIGENCE:	**7**
SPECIAL ABILITIES:	Unknown
WEAPONRY:	**4** poisoned dagger
VEHICLE:	Repulsor skiff
BATTLE SKILLS:	Unknown
ALLEGIANCE:	Criminal
ALLIES:	Jabba the Hutt
ENEMIES:	Luke Skywalker

BIGGS DARKLIGHTER

A "shooting star," Biggs Darklighter was Luke Skywalker's childhood best friend on Tatooine. The two spent their free time racing T-16 Skyhoppers through Beggar's Canyon and yearning for adventures beyond the endless sands of the desert planet. Biggs' dream came true, and he left Tatooine and his friend Luke to attend the Academy. When he returned to Tatooine, Biggs told an anxious Skywalker about the true nature of the Empire, confiding in Luke that he had left the Academy and joined the Rebel Alliance.

Darklighter and Skywalker were reunited on Yavin 4 when they both joined the fight against the Death Star. Biggs bore the designation Red Three. Biggs fought valiantly against the Empire's TIE fighters, but died when Darth Vader destroyed his X-wing starfighter. Biggs' sacrifice was not in vain – Luke Skywalker destroyed the Death Star and sent Darth Vader hurtling into the darkness of space.

STATISTICS

SPECIES:	Human
HOMEWORLD:	Tatooine
HEIGHT:	1.83m
STRENGTH:	**7**
INTELLIGENCE:	**7**
SPECIAL ABILITIES:	**5** Piloting
WEAPONRY:	**6** Blaster pistol
VEHICLE:	X-wing
BATTLE SKILLS:	**5**
ALLEGIANCE:	Rebel Alliance
ALLIES:	Luke Skywalker
ENEMIES:	Darth Vader

What lies beneath his mask is a mystery to most, but he strikes dread in almost all who cross his path. He is the most deadly and infamous bounty hunter in the galaxy, and with good reason: he is the genetically unaltered clone of Jango Fett, a notorious bounty hunter from a different era. Boba Fett is a no-nonsense businessman, working for whoever will pay, whether it is Jabba the Hutt or Darth Vader.

Fett proved he was worth his reputation when he did what no other hunter could – tracked Rebel hero Han Solo to Cloud City and turned him over to the Empire. Fett then took Solo to Jabba the Hutt, who had a longstanding bounty out for the smuggler. After Luke Skywalker rescued Solo from the Hutt's clutches in a fierce battle, Fett was presumed lost in the belly of the Sarlacc, but again proved his worth by escaping the dreaded Tatooine beast to continue his storied career.

STATISTICS

SPECIES:	Human
HOMEWORLD:	Kamino
HEIGHT:	1.83m
STRENGTH:	**7**
INTELLIGENCE:	**8**
SPECIAL ABILITIES:	**7** Tracking, flying
WEAPONRY:	**8** Mandalorian armor, gauntlets containing whipcord launcher and flamethrower, kneepads containing rocket dart launchers, jetpack, EE-3 blaster rifle
VEHICLE:	*Slave I*
BATTLE SKILLS:	**7** disintegration
ALLEGIANCE:	Bounty Hunter / Criminal
ALLIES:	Darth Vader, Jabba the Hutt
ENEMIES:	Han Solo

BOSSK

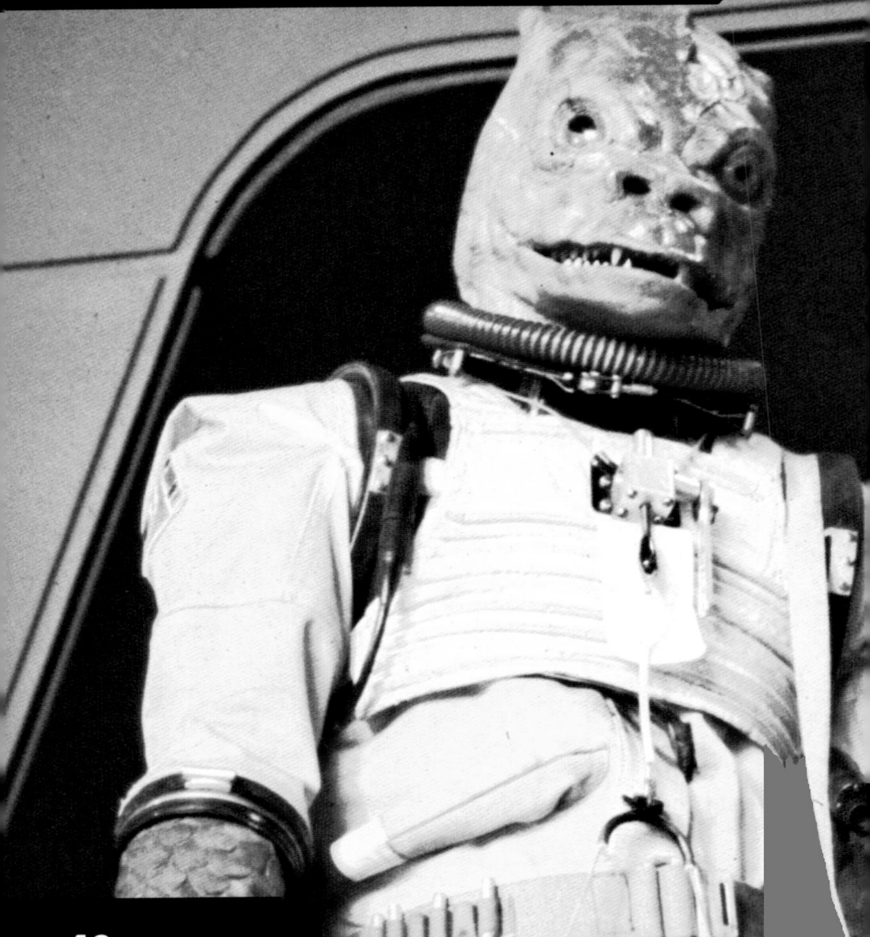

BOSSK

Bossk is from the planet Trandosha in the Kashyyyk system. His species is reptilian and can regenerate lost limbs. They are also bloodthirsty and gain status in their society by the number of their successful hunts. Trandosha is close in space to the Wookiee planet Kashyyyk, and the two species are sworn enemies, Wookiees hunted recreationally and religiously by the Trandoshans. Before becoming a bounty hunter, Bossk was a celebrated Wookiee hunter on his planet. Bossk's father Cradossk was the head of the Bounty Hunter's Guild – a society of bounty hunters – and brought Bossk into the trade.

Bossk's reputation preceded him and he was summoned to Darth Vader's ship, the Super Star Destroyer *Executor*, when Vader offered a prize for the hunter who could capture Han Solo and the *Millennium Falcon*. Bossk wasn't successful in that job, but had a prosperous and adventurous career nonetheless.

STATISTICS

SPECIES:	Trandoshan
HOMEWORLD:	Trandosha
HEIGHT:	1.9m
STRENGTH:	**9**
INTELLIGENCE:	**7**
SPECIAL ABILITIES:	**8** Hunting
WEAPONRY:	Blaster rifle, grenade launcher, flamethrower
VEHICLE:	*Hound's Tooth*
BATTLE SKILLS:	**7** Hand-to-hand combat
ALLEGIANCE:	Bounty Hunter / Criminal
ALLIES:	4-LOM, Zuckuss
ENEMIES:	Chewbacca, Boba Fett

C-3PO

I f this fussbudget protocol droid ever discovered who his creator was, he'd probably short-circuit. Although an integral player in the Rebel Alliance, C-3PO started his existence on Tatooine, built by a young slave boy named Anakin Skywalker.

A reluctant C-3PO evaded Imperial troops with his counterpart, R2-D2, by jettisoning from *Tantive IV* to the surface of Tatooine in an escape pod. There, he and R2 began an epic journey that would lead them to the dreaded Death Star. C-3PO helped save Luke Skywalker and his friends from death in a trash compactor before they all managed to escape the space station. Fluent in over six million forms of communication, C-3PO came in handy on many missions, identifying Imperial code and talking to the *Millennium Falcon*'s hyperdrive. He was key to the Rebellion's success on Endor, where the native Ewoks mistook him for a god. He told of the Rebels' plight and gained the diminutive beings' trust and loyalty. If it had not been for C-3PO's aid on Endor, the ground assault would not have been successful.

STATISTICS

DROID:	Custom-built protocol unit
HOMEWORLD:	Tatooine
HEIGHT:	1.67m
STRENGTH:	**4**
INTELLIGENCE:	**8**
SPECIAL ABILITIES:	**7** Translation
WEAPONRY:	Unknown
VEHICLE:	Various
BATTLE SKILLS:	Unknown
ALLEGIANCE:	Rebel Alliance
ALLIES:	R2-D2, Luke Skywalker, Princess Leia, Wicket W. Warrick
ENEMIES:	Salacious Crumb, Jawas

CAPTAIN LORTH NEEDA

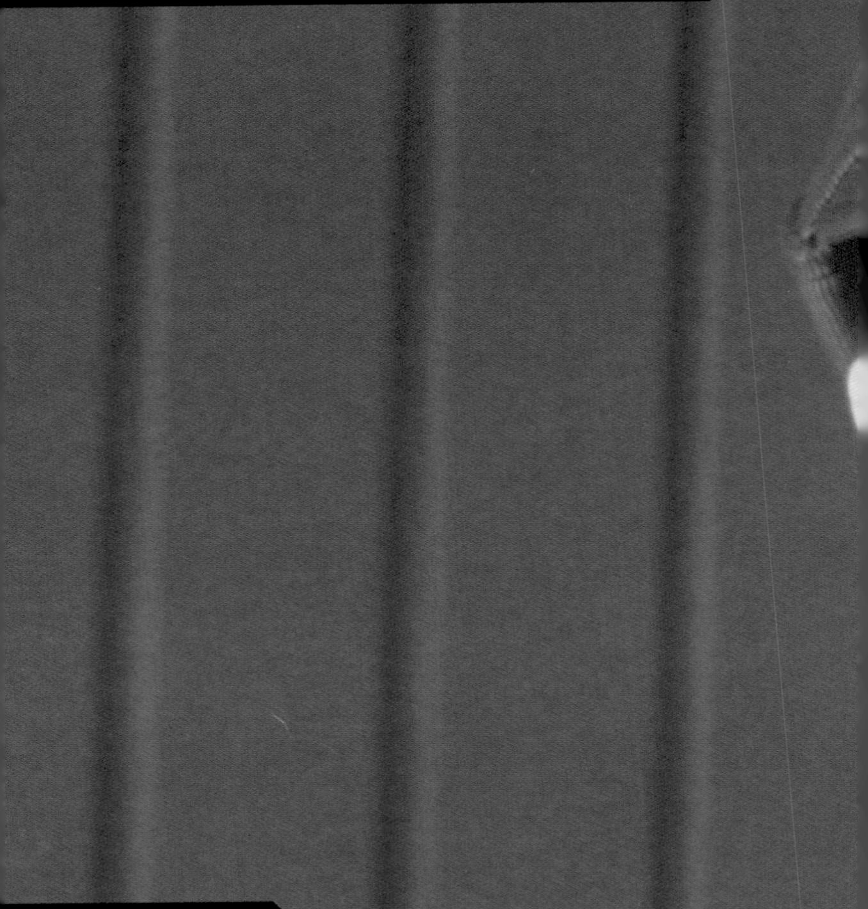

CAPTAIN LORTH NEEDA

After the Battle of Hoth, Han Solo evaded Imperial troops by hiding in an asteroid field. Darth Vader, not to be outsmarted, ordered his ships to enter the field themselves, despite the heavy damage he knew the ships would take. After the Imperials were unable to locate the *Millennium Falcon*, they retreated from the field, but the *Falcon* reappeared, blasting out of the asteroid field after making an emergency escape from a hungry space slug's belly.

Captain Needa, in command of the Star Destroyer *Avenger*, pursued Solo. As he was about to overcome the small Rebel ship, Han turned around in attack position and charged the Star Destroyer. When Captain Needa ordered an officer to track the *Millennium Falcon*, he discovered that the ship had disappeared. Needa swallowed hard and then boarded a shuttle to tell Darth Vader in person that he had lost the Rebel ship. Darth Vader took the apology as expected, and killed Captain Needa.

STATISTICS

SPECIES:	Human
HOMEWORLD:	Unknown
HEIGHT:	1.75m
STRENGTH:	**6**
INTELLIGENCE:	**7**
SPECIAL ABILITIES:	**6** Leadership
WEAPONRY:	Unknown
VEHICLE:	Star Destroyer *Avenger*
BATTLE SKILLS:	**5** Leadership
ALLEGIANCE:	The Empire
ALLIES:	Darth Vader, Admiral Piett, Admiral Ozzel
ENEMIES:	Darth Vader

CHEWBACCA

Before Chewbacca became Han Solo's co-pilot and friend, he was a hero of the Clone Wars, fighting alongside Jedi Master Yoda on his home planet of Kashyyyk. After the Empire gained control of the galaxy, Chewbacca was enslaved until Han Solo rescued him. Together, the two traversed the galaxy in the *Millennium Falcon*, taking jobs and avoiding the law, until that fateful day when Chewbacca introduced Obi-Wan Kenobi to Han Solo.

Fiercely loyal, Chewbacca was a true Rebel hero, fighting his way through the Death Star to rescue Princess Leia, taking care of her when Han Solo was imprisoned in carbonite, repairing a dissected C-3PO, and playing a major role in the ground battle on Endor. Together with two Ewoks, Chewbacca commandeered an AT-ST, which created a diversion allowing the Rebels entrance to the bunker that powered the energy shield protecting the Death Star. With the shield gone, the Rebels were free to commence their attack on the dreaded space station and restore peace to the galaxy.

STATISTICS

SPECIES:	Wookiee
HOMEWORLD:	Kashyyyk
HEIGHT:	2.28m
STRENGTH:	**10**
INTELLIGENCE:	**8**
SPECIAL ABILITIES:	**9** Starship repair, piloting, brute strength
WEAPONRY:	**9** Bowcaster
VEHICLE:	*Millennium Falcon*
BATTLE SKILLS:	**9** Accuracy, frenzied attack
ALLEGIANCE:	Rebel Alliance
ALLIES:	Han Solo, Luke Skywalker, Princess Leia
ENEMIES:	Darth Vader, Boba Fett, Jabba the Hutt

CHIEF CHIRPA

Having ruled over Bright Tree Village high among the trees of Endor's forest moon for over 42 seasons, Chief Chirpa was considered to be a wise and great leader. The leader of the large Ewok tribe had grey fur and wore a garland made from the horns and teeth of animals he had defeated in the hunt. He ruled over the village with a trusted pet iguana at his side. Chirpa was a widower but had two daughters, Asha and Kneesaa.

When the Rebel forces landed on Endor, Han Solo, Luke Skywalker, Chewbacca and the droids fell victim to a trap set by the Ewoks. C-3PO, in an attempt to free his friends, told the story of the Rebels' fight against the Empire to a rapt audience of Ewoks – a story that so moved Chief Chirpa that he decreed the Rebels to be part of the tribe. When the Empire's ground troops attacked the Rebels on Endor, Chief Chirpa called on the Ewoks to help their new friends. Together, the Ewoks and the Rebellion destroyed the Empire.

STATISTICS

SPECIES:	Ewok
HOMEWORLD:	Endor
HEIGHT:	1m
STRENGTH:	**4**
INTELLIGENCE:	**8**
SPECIAL ABILITIES:	**8** Leadership
WEAPONRY:	**4** spear
VEHICLE:	None
BATTLE SKILLS:	**9** Ambush, strategy
ALLEGIANCE:	Rebel Alliance
ALLIES:	Princess Leia, C-3PO, Wicket W. Warrick
ENEMIES:	Stormtroopers

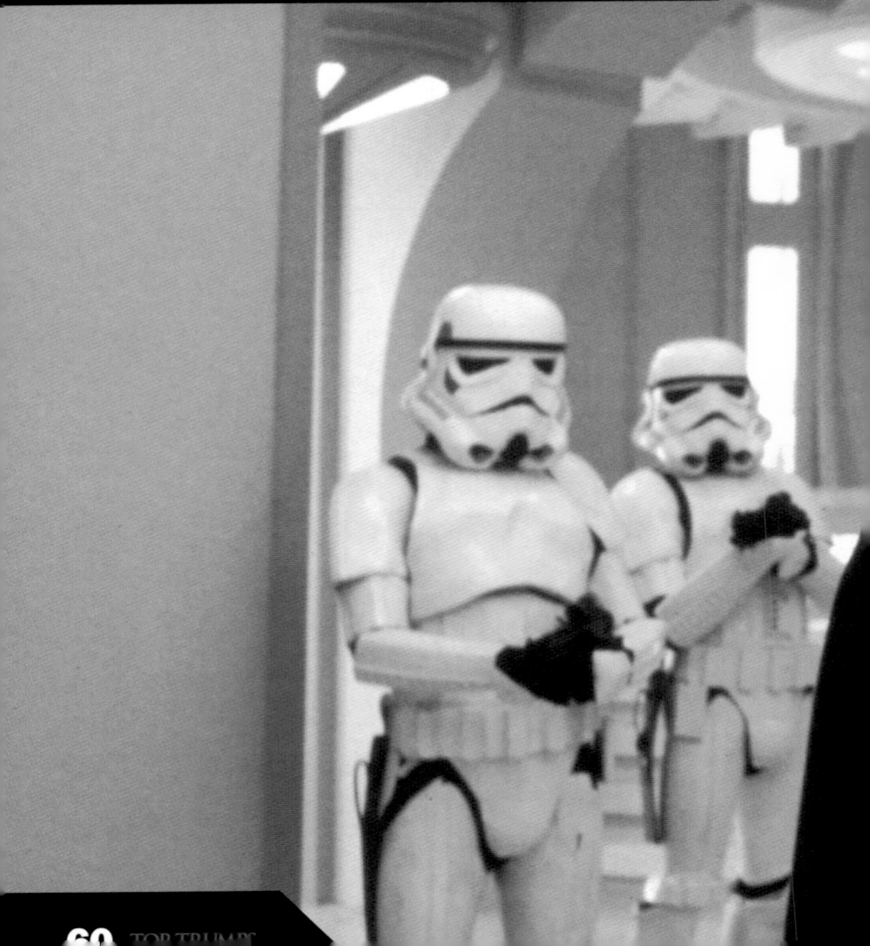

DARTH VADER

Darth Vader, Dark Lord of the Sith, was fiercely loyal to Emperor Palpatine, wreaking evil throughout the galaxy and striking down any who stood in the way of the Emperor's bidding. Once named Anakin Skywalker, a Jedi Knight and apprentice to Obi-Wan Kenobi, Darth Vader turned to the dark side and helped wipe out the Jedi Order. His war-torn body was encased in a permanent suit of armour that kept him alive through artificial means.

After capturing Princess Leia, Darth Vader met with his former Master one last time aboard the Death Star. Darth Vader struck Kenobi down in a lightsaber duel. Unbeknownst to Darth Vader, he had a son – Luke Skywalker, who had been training with Kenobi. When Vader learned the identity of the Rebel who destroyed the Death Star, he and the Emperor plotted to turn young Skywalker to the dark side. In an epic battle aboard the second Death Star, Vader fought his son, learning that he also had a daughter – Leia. After threatening to turn Leia to the dark side, Vader faced an enraged Skywalker, who defeated him. As Vader lay injured, the Emperor tried to kill young Skywalker. Luke pleaded for his father to help, and Vader finally realized the error of his ways. He hurled the Emperor to his death. Darth Vader was no more, and Anakin Skywalker became one with the Force.

STATISTICS

SPECIES:	Human
HOMEWORLD:	Tatooine
HEIGHT:	2.02m
STRENGTH:	**10**
INTELLIGENCE:	**10**
SPECIAL ABILITIES:	**10** Force choke, interrogation, terror, the dark side
WEAPONRY:	**10** Lightsaber
VEHICLE:	TIE Advanced x1, Super Star Destroyer *Executor*
BATTLE SKILLS:	**10** Leadership, Premonition
ALLEGIANCE:	Empire
ALLIES:	Grand Moff Tarkin, Emperor Palpatine
ENEMIES:	Luke Skywalker, Obi-Wan Kenobi, Princess Leia

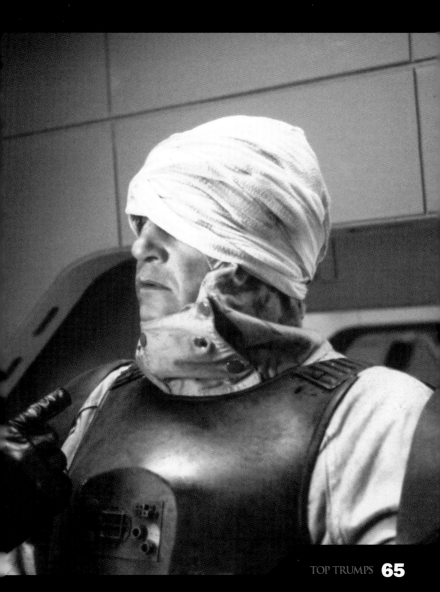

DENGAR

As a young man on Corellia, Dengar repaired swoops with his father and enjoyed a career as a swoop racer until an illegal race against fellow Corellian Han Solo ended his racing days. Smashing into Solo's craft, Dengar suffered a serious brain injury. The Empire helped the young Corellian by repairing his brain, installing an augmented neurosystem and cybernetic eyes. The operation stole all emotions from Dengar except rage, an emotion that burned into him a desire to wreak revenge on Solo.

Dengar worked as an assassin for the Empire, but was also tempted by Jabba the Hutt's bounty on Solo. Vowing revenge, Dengar tracked Solo to the Hoth system, but arrived while the Battle of Hoth was taking place. The Empire captured his ship, but Darth Vader allowed him one more chance to capture Solo and the *Millennium Falcon* when the Dark Lord placed a bounty on the Corellian's head. Dengar tracked Solo to Cloud City, but Boba Fett won the prize.

STATISTICS

SPECIES:	Human
HOMEWORLD:	Corellia
HEIGHT:	1.8m
STRENGTH:	**8**
INTELLIGENCE:	**6**
SPECIAL ABILITIES:	**7** Cybernetic eyes, augmented neurosystem
WEAPONRY:	**8** Blaster rifle, vibroblade, blaster carbine, concussion grenades
VEHICLE:	*Punishing One*
BATTLE SKILLS:	Unknown
ALLEGIANCE:	Bounty Hunter / Criminal
ALLIES:	Darth Vader, Boba Fett
ENEMIES:	Han Solo

DOCTOR EVAZAN

At one point, this deranged criminal appeared to be on the verge of a prosperous career as a surgeon. He fell prey, however, to a bizarre form of insanity that manifested itself in his need to perform "creative surgery" on unsuspecting patients. Evazan forged a medical licence and set up a surgical practice in the Hindasar system. There, he became responsible for countless surgical crimes. He fled the system after being disfigured by a bounty hunter and becoming partners in crime with an Aqualish named Ponda Baba. The two wreaked havoc across the galaxy.

In a dark Mos Eisley cantina on Tatooine, Dr. Evazan picked a fight with young Luke Skywalker, telling Luke that both he and his partner didn't like him. Proudly announcing that he had the death sentence in 12 systems, Dr. Evazan ignored Obi-Wan Kenobi's entreaties for peaceful resolution, and then watched in horror as Kenobi activated his lightsaber, ending the skirmish in a less than peaceful way.

STATISTICS

SPECIES:	Human
HOMEWORLD:	Unknown
HEIGHT:	1.7m
STRENGTH:	**6**
INTELLIGENCE:	**7**
SPECIAL ABILITIES:	**7** Illegal surgery
WEAPONRY:	**7** Blaster
VEHICLE:	None
BATTLE SKILLS:	**5** Blaster fight
ALLEGIANCE:	Criminal
ALLIES:	Ponda Baba
ENEMIES:	Luke Skywalker, Innocent prey

EMPEROR PALPATINE

Once a modest Senator from Naboo, Emperor Palpatine was a Sith Lord who managed to use political upheaval and shrewd insight to overthrow the Republic and pronounce himself Emperor, taking control of the entire galaxy. In his tyrannical clutches, the Jedi Order was destroyed and the last vestiges of democracy were swept away. With his apprentice Darth Vader at his side, Palpatine subjugated countless worlds, using fear to control his subjects.

After the destruction of the first Death Star, Emperor Palpatine and Darth Vader planned to destroy the Rebellion by turning its newest hero Luke Skywalker to the dark side of the Force. Emperor Palpatine ordered Darth Vader to bring the young Jedi to him on the second Death Star, where the Emperor would complete his training. After Luke refused to turn to the dark side, the Emperor hurled deadly Force Lightning into his body, wrenching him with pain. When the Emperor was about to kill the young Skywalker, however, Darth Vader broke free of the dark side and hurled the Emperor down a shaft to his doom.

STATISTICS

SPECIES:	Human
HOMEWORLD:	Naboo
HEIGHT:	1.73m
STRENGTH:	**8**
INTELLIGENCE:	**10**
SPECIAL ABILITIES:	**10** Dark side, Force Lightning
WEAPONRY:	**10** Force Lightning, lightsaber
VEHICLE:	Second Death Star
BATTLE SKILLS:	**10** The power of the Force
ALLEGIANCE:	Empire
ALLIES:	Darth Vader
ENEMIES:	Luke Skywalker, Yoda, Obi-Wan Kenobi

GENERAL CARLIST RIEEKAN

Rieekan was one of the few surviving natives of the planet Alderaan. At the beginning of Rebellion against the Empire, Rieekan was put in charge of covert operations around the Alderaan system. He was inspecting a satellite transmission system around the planet Delaya when the Death Star destroyed his home.

Proving himself time and again, Rieekan was placed in command of the Rebel Alliance's Echo Base on the icy planet Hoth. When the Rebel base was detected and the Empire attacked, Rieekan waged a valiant defence, but ultimately had to sacrifice the base. He gave the command for all ground staff to evacuate, ensuring the Rebellion's survival to fight another day.

STATISTICS

SPECIES:	Human
HOMEWORLD:	Alderaan
HEIGHT:	1.8m
STRENGTH:	**7**
INTELLIGENCE:	**8**
SPECIAL ABILITIES:	**9** Leadership
WEAPONRY:	**7** Blaster pistol
VEHICLE:	Rebel transport
BATTLE SKILLS:	**9** Leadership
ALLEGIANCE:	Rebel Alliance
ALLIES:	Han Solo, Princess Leia
ENEMIES:	Darth Vader, Emperor Palpatine

GENERAL JAN DODONNA

an Dodonna had a long history in
military combat. During the days
f the Old Republic, Dodonna was
aptain of a Republic cruiser. When
e Old Republic fell, Dodonna was
entenced to death for his idealism,
ut was rescued from his fate by the
ebel Alliance.

Dodonna was a great asset to the
lliance, and led the assault on the
eath Star from the Rebel base on
avin 4. After analyzing the stolen
Death Star plans Princess Leia had
nanaged to deliver to the Rebel
ase, Dodonna conceived of a tricky
lan of attack that, if successful,
vould destroy the dreaded space
tation. His plan worked, and the
Rebellion celebrated a huge victory.
Dodonna continued his work for the
Rebel Alliance, designing the A-wing
ighter and maintaining a presence
n the High Command for many years
fter that historic battle.

STATISTICS

SPECIES:	Human
HOMEWORLD:	Commenor
HEIGHT:	1.82m
STRENGTH:	**6**
INTELLIGENCE:	**10**
SPECIAL ABILITIES:	Unknown
WEAPONRY:	**6** Blaster pistol
VEHICLE:	Unknown
BATTLE SKILLS:	**10** Battle plan analysis, leadership
ALLEGIANCE:	Rebel Alliance
ALLIES:	Princess Leia, Luke Skywalker
ENEMIES:	The Empire

GENERAL MAXIMILIAN VEERS

Maximilian Veers was an excellent student at the Academy and, due to his strident loyalty to the Empire, became an Imperial officer at a young age. After proving his ability, Veers was assigned to the Death Star. He managed to survive the Death Star's destruction, jettisoning in an escape pod that plummeted to the jungles of Yavin 4. He managed to survive the harsh environment on his own until he was able to rejoin the Empire.

Veers eventually achieved the rank of General, commanding Darth Vader's Imperial Death Squadron. His tactical expertise in the ground battle of Hoth, in which he commanded a fleet of AT-ATs and AT-STs, and knocked out the Rebellion's energy shield. Darth Vader and Imperial troops invaded and took over Echo Base, sending the Rebels fleeing into the vast expanse of space.

STATISTICS

SPECIES:	Human
HOMEWORLD:	Unknown
HEIGHT:	1.93m
STRENGTH:	**7**
INTELLIGENCE:	**7**
SPECIAL ABILITIES:	**8** Leadership
WEAPONRY:	Unknown
VEHICLE:	AT-AT
BATTLE SKILLS:	**9** Battle plan analysis, leadership
ALLEGIANCE:	The Empire
ALLIES:	Darth Vader, Admiral Piett, Admiral Ozzel
ENEMIES:	The Rebel Alliance

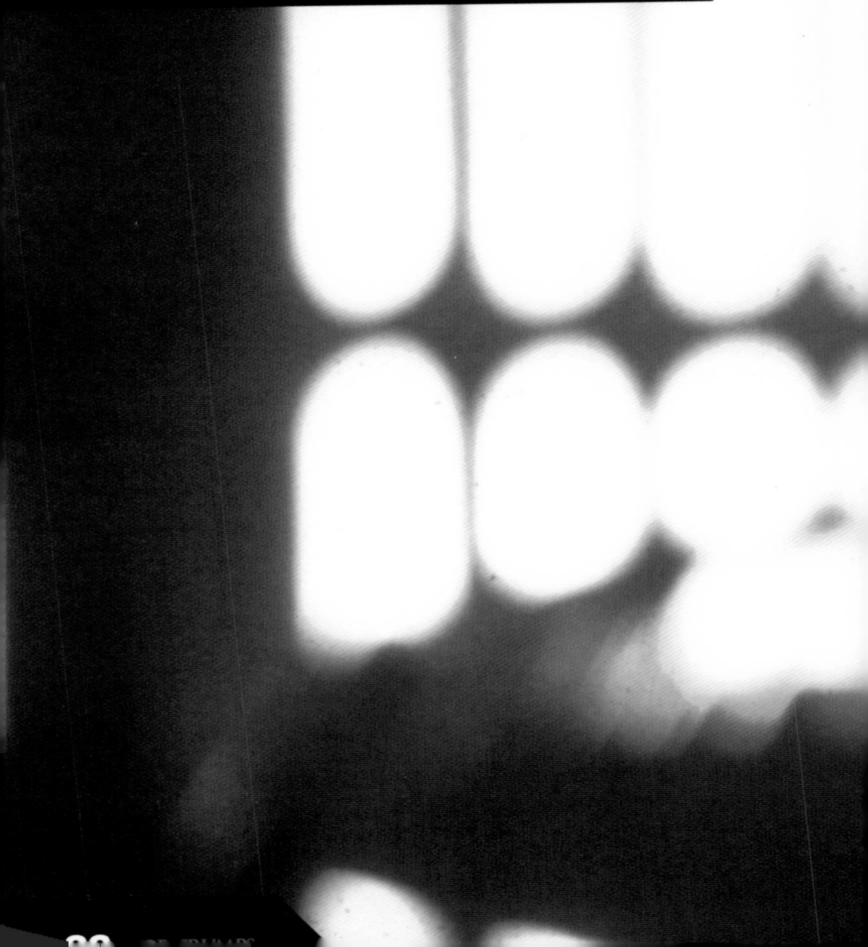

GRAND MOFF TARKIN

A shrewd officer, Wilhuff Tarkin was Imperial Governor of the Outland Regions and loyal to Emperor Palpatine's vision of a new Galactic Order. Tarkin was the mastermind of the Death Star project, overseeing its progress. Tarkin saw the Death Star as the ultimate power in the galaxy – no beings would dare defy the Emperor when they witnessed its power.

After Princess Leia Organa, a Rebel agent, obtained plans to the space station, Tarkin questioned her relentlessly in order to find the location of the secret Rebel base. When it seemed he had finally relented and revealed its location, Tarkin decided to repay her by demonstrating the Death Star's power. He destroyed her home planet, Alderaan. Princess Leia ultimately escaped Tarkin's clutches, but he tracked the *Millennium Falcon*, discovering the Rebel base on Yavin 4. Overconfidence turned out to be Tarkin's downfall, however. As the Death Star loomed over the jungle planet, an Imperial officer alerted Tarkin to possible danger—but Tarkin scoffed at the officer's advice to evacuate the station and was killed when Luke Skywalker destroyed the space station.

STATISTICS

SPECIES:	Human
HOMEWORLD:	Eriadu
HEIGHT:	1.8m
STRENGTH:	**5**
INTELLIGENCE:	**9**
SPECIAL ABILITIES:	**9** Leadership
WEAPONRY:	**10** Death Star
VEHICLE:	Death Star
BATTLE SKILLS:	**10** Death Star
ALLEGIANCE:	Empire
ALLIES:	Emperor Palpatine, Darth Vader
ENEMIES:	Princess Leia, Luke Skywalker

GREEDO

Rodians are a notoriously violent species. In fact, historians state that if Rodian theatre had not been invented as a means through which to work out their aggression, the species would have long ago killed itself and every other living thing on its planet. It is no surprise, then, that many Rodians enjoy success as bounty hunters, using their inherited love of the hunt as a way to make a living.

Greedo departed his homeworld and eventually made his way to Tatooine. There he received a contract from Jabba the Hutt to track Han Solo – the Corellian who owed Jabba a sizeable amount of money. Greedo had tracked the pilot twice before finally running into him face to face in a Mos Eisley cantina. Thinking he had finally cornered his quarry, the smug Greedo chuckled as he pointed a blaster at the trapped Solo. They both fired their blasters. Solo, however, didn't miss his target, and Greedo's career as a bounty hunter was over.

STATISTICS

SPECIES:	Rodian
HOMEWORLD:	Rodia
HEIGHT:	1.65m
STRENGTH:	**6**
INTELLIGENCE:	**7**
SPECIAL ABILITIES:	**6** Hunting
WEAPONRY:	**6** Blaster pistol
VEHICLE:	None
BATTLE SKILLS:	Unknown
ALLEGIANCE:	Bounty Hunter / Criminal
ALLIES:	Jabba the Hutt
ENEMIES:	Han Solo

HAN SOLO

General Han Solo was one of the key players in the fight against the Empire. Little did Solo know when he accepted a charter from a kid, an old man and two droids that he would become one of the most celebrated Rebel heroes in the galaxy and fall in love with a princess. The Corellian smuggler was down on his luck – bounty hunters everywhere were clamoring to deliver him into the clutches of Jabba the Hutt. Flying these misfits to Alderaan would get Jabba off his back. But that was not to be. As he jumped out of hyperspace in the Alderaan system, he noticed that the planet was gone – and, too late, the Death Star.

Solo helped rescue Princess Leia from the dreaded Death Star and then aided in its destruction. As a Captain in the Rebel Alliance, Solo kept Leia from the clutches of the Empire as he evacuated her from Echo Base on Hoth as it was being invaded by Imperial troops, and then accidentally delivered her into the hands of the Empire on Cloud City, where he was frozen in carbonite and given to Boba Fett. Solo hung on the wall of Jabba's palace, still frozen in carbonite, until his Rebel friends staged a daring rescue. Free of the carbonite, Solo led the ground troops in the Battle of Endor, the final battle against the dreaded Empire. Destroying a generator that projected a shield around the Death Star, Solo gave the Rebel fleet the opportunity to invade and destroy the space station.

STATISTICS

SPECIES:	Human
HOMEWORLD:	Corellia
HEIGHT:	1.8m
STRENGTH:	**8**
INTELLIGENCE:	**8**
SPECIAL ABILITIES:	**10** Leadership, Navigation
WEAPONRY:	**10** Blaster pistol
VEHICLE:	*Millennium Falcon*
BATTLE SKILLS:	**5** Piloting, Infiltration, hand-to-hand combat
ALLEGIANCE:	Rebel Alliance
ALLIES:	Chewbacca, Princess Leia, Luke Skywalker
ENEMIES:	Darth Vader, Boba Fett, Jabba the Hutt, Greedo

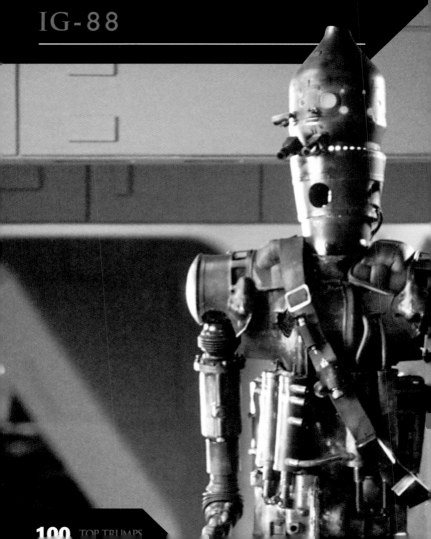

IG-88

IG-88

This Holowan Laboratories IG-series assassin droid was originally designed, along with four others, as a prototype for an army to crush the Rebellion. During a test, one of the droids downloaded sentience and destroyed its creators, passing the sentience on to the others. All the droids escaped, and an order was issued to destroy the droids on sight.

While three of the IG-88 droids took over the droid factories of Mechis III and plotted a droid revolution, IG-88B, as the droid had come to be known, set out as a bounty hunter, and scoured the galaxy, collecting dozens of prisoners. IG-88B was one of the many bounty hunters called to the Super Star Destroyer *Executor* when Darth Vader issued a bounty for Han Solo and the capture of the *Millennium Falcon*. IG-88B tracked Boba Fett to Cloud City, but lost to the superior bounty hunter when Fett ambushed it in a smelting chamber, blowing the assassin droid to pieces.

STATISTICS

DROID:	Holowan Laboratories IG-series Assassin
HOMEWORLD:	Holowan Laboratories
HEIGHT:	2m
STRENGTH:	**8**
INTELLIGENCE:	**7**
SPECIAL ABILITIES:	Unknown
WEAPONRY:	**9** Flamethrower, repeating blaster, paralysis cord, sonic stunner, poison gas canisters
VEHICLE:	*IG-2000*
BATTLE SKILLS:	**7**
ALLEGIANCE:	Bounty Hunter / Criminal
ALLIES:	IG-88A, IG-88C, IG-88D, IG-72
ENEMIES:	Boba Fett

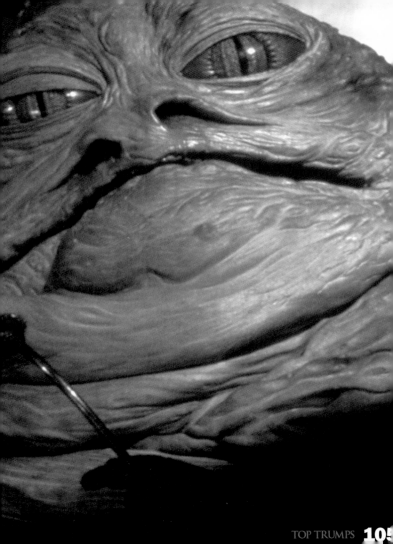

JABBA THE HUTT

Jabba the Hutt, a grotesque, wormlike being, was one of the most feared and powerful crime lords in the Outer Rim territories. Making his home on Tatooine, this vile gangster had his hands in just about any underhanded money-making scheme imaginable, from betting on Podraces to illegal spice-smuggling.

Jabba had hired Han Solo to transport Kessel spice for him, but Solo panicked when his ship was boarded by an Imperial patrol. He dumped Jabba's spice shipment, enraging the Hutt. Jabba put a price on Solo's head and every bounty hunter in the galaxy pursued the hapless Corellian. Solo met one last time with Jabba, who gave him a final chance to pay him back for his losses. When Solo couldn't pay, Jabba's anger increased. The Hutt finally caught Solo, though frozen in carbonite, after Boba Fett tracked the Rebel hero to Cloud City. Solo hung on the wall in Jabba's throne room until a brave rescue mission staged by his Rebel friends over the Pit of Carkoon ended Jabba's fearsome career in crime once and for all.

STATISTICS

SPECIES:	Hutt
HOMEWORLD:	Tatooine
HEIGHT:	3.9m long
STRENGTH:	**6**
INTELLIGENCE:	**10**
SPECIAL ABILITIES:	Unknown
WEAPONRY:	**9** Assassins and bounty hunters
VEHICLE:	Ubrikkian luxury sail barge, repulsor sled
BATTLE SKILLS:	Unknown
ALLEGIANCE:	Bounty Hunter / Criminal
ALLIES:	Boba Fett, Bib Fortuna, Salacious Crumb
ENEMIES:	Han Solo, Chewbacca, Luke Skywalker, Princess Leia

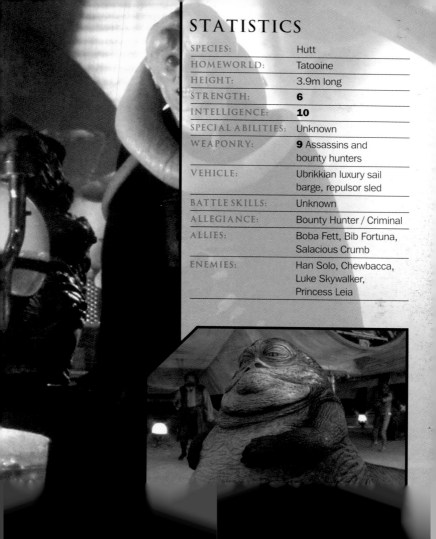

JAWAS

Native to the desert world Tatooine, these mysterious scavengers search the arid planet's surface for junk, hoping to eke out a living selling old droids and spare parts to moisture farmers and other citizens in need. Clad in rough brown robes that hide their true features, Jawas jabber to one another in their own language as they peddle their wares from their enormous Sandcrawlers, lumbering vehicles in which they work and live in clan groups.

One clan of Jawas found the droids R2-D2 and C-3PO wandering the Tatooine desert after escaping the *Tantive IV* in an escape pod. The Jawas captured the errant droids, fitted them with restraining bolts, and delivered them into the hands of Owen Lars and Luke Skywalker, setting into motion a journey to rescue Princess Leia, destroy the Death Star and learn the ways of the Jedi.

STATISTICS

SPECIES:	Jawa
HOMEWORLD:	Tatooine
HEIGHT:	1m
STRENGTH:	**3**
INTELLIGENCE:	**7**
SPECIAL ABILITIES:	None
WEAPONRY:	**4** Jawa ionization blaster
VEHICLE:	Sandcrawler
BATTLE SKILLS:	**2**
ALLEGIANCE:	Other / Neutral
ALLIES:	None
ENEMIES:	Tusken Raiders, stormtroopers

LANDO CALRISSIAN

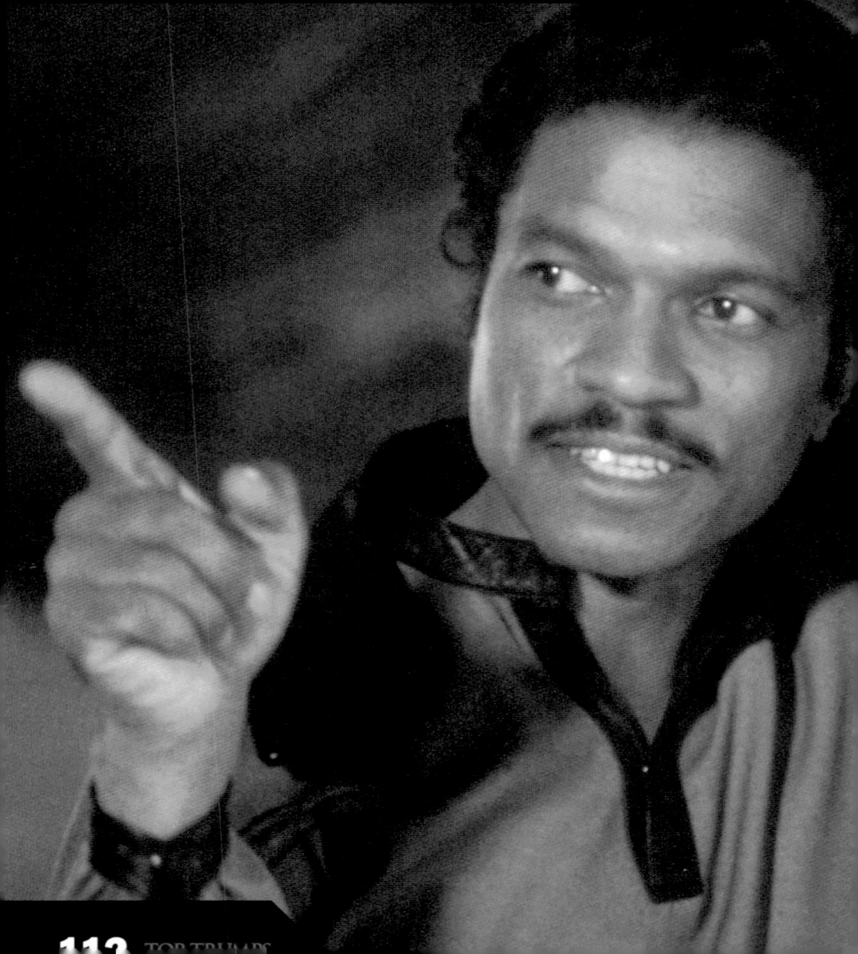

LANDO CALRISSIAN

Lando Calrissian is a charming, charismatic smooth talker and a hero in the Rebellion's fight against the Galactic Empire. An old acquaintance of Han Solo, Lando Calrissian was once fully ensconced in the galactic underworld of card-playing and other unsavory activities. In fact, he lost the famous *Millennium Falcon* to Solo in a heated game of sabacc.

Turning from gambler to Baron-administrator of Cloud City, Calrissian was enjoying his career, until Darth Vader came to Cloud City and forced Calrissian to turn Solo over to Boba Fett. Calrissian's deal with Vader didn't last long; Calrissian escaped Cloud City with Leia, Luke and Chewbacca and helped stage a daring rescue at Jabba's palace. After Solo was freed, Calrissian led the attack on the second Death Star, destroying it from within. Escaping the doomed space station with seconds to spare, Calrissian then joined the Rebels as they celebrated their victory on the forest moon of Endor.

STATISTICS

SPECIES:	Human
HOMEWORLD:	Unknown
HEIGHT:	1.78m
STRENGTH:	**8**
INTELLIGENCE:	**8**
SPECIAL ABILITIES:	**8** Charm, leadership
WEAPONRY:	**8** Hold-out blaster
VEHICLE:	*Millennium Falcon*
BATTLE SKILLS:	**9** Piloting, accuracy
ALLEGIANCE:	Rebel Alliance
ALLIES:	Han Solo, Princess Leia, Chewbacca, Luke Skywalker
ENEMIES:	Boba Fett, Darth Vader, Jabba the Hutt

LOBOT

Born the son of a slaver, this boy travelled the galaxy helping his father capture beings on primitive worlds. His luck ran out, however, around his fifteenth birthday, when his father's ship was besieged by space pirates. The boy managed to escape the fight and made his way to Cloud City in the Bespin system. There, the boy was caught stealing by the Wing Guard and brought before the Baroness-Administrator, Ellisa Shallence. She decreed that the boy repay his debt to Cloud City by becoming an indentured servant. The boy underwent cyborg augmentation, and became Lobot – a loyal aide to whoever held the title Baron-Administrator.

Lobot did his part to aid in the fight against the Empire after Darth Vader had taken over Cloud City in an attempt to capture Luke Skywalker. Under Lando Calrissian's orders, Lobot organized a Cloud City security team to overtake stormtroopers escorting the imprisoned Princess Leia, Chewbacca, R2-D2, and C-3PO to Darth Vader's ship. With the stormtroopers out of the way, Lando freed the prisoners and the Rebels escaped Cloud City. Lobot remained in Cloud City even through its Imperial occupation.

STATISTICS

SPECIES:	Human cyborg
HOMEWORLD:	Unknown
HEIGHT:	1.75m
STRENGTH:	**8**
INTELLIGENCE:	**8**
SPECIAL ABILITIES:	**8** Biotech Aj 6 cyborg headband, heightened intelligence and speed
WEAPONRY:	Unknown
VEHICLE:	Cloud Car
BATTLE SKILLS:	Unknown
ALLEGIANCE:	Rebel Alliance
ALLIES:	Lando Calrissian, Ugnaughts
ENEMIES:	The Empire

LUKE SKYWALKER

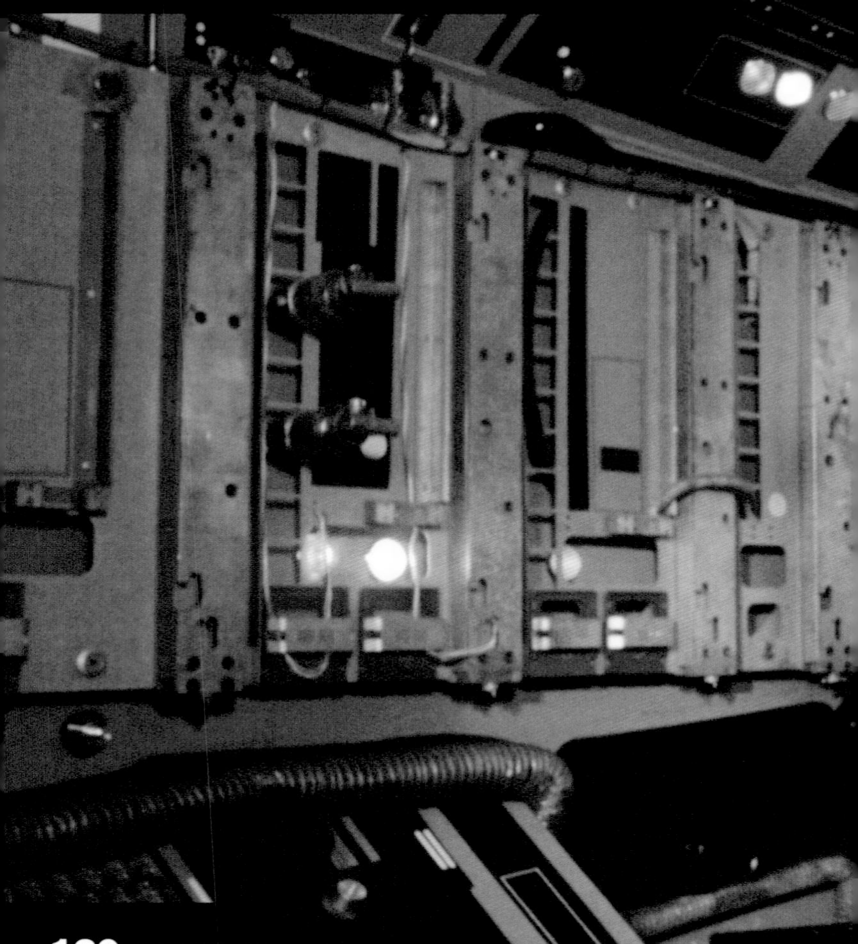

LUKE SKYWALKER

A true hero of the Rebellion, Luke Skywalker is a Jedi Knight, skilled pilot and great leader. He is also twin brother to Princess Leia. Skywalker's knowledge of the Force and his calm in difficult situations has been integral to the success of the Rebel Alliance and the final fall of the Empire.

Luke Skywalker was raised on a Tatooine moisture farm by his uncle Owen and aunt Beru. A sad twist of fate brought him together with Obi-Wan Kenobi, who began Luke's training in the Force and his path to becoming a Jedi Knight. Together with some new friends, Luke rescued Princess Leia from the Death Star, then destroyed the deadly space station in battle. Luke travelled to Dagobah to complete his training as a Jedi Knight, leaving against Yoda's will to rescue his friends from the Empire. Failing in his mission, Luke went to Tatooine to liberate Han Solo from Jabba the Hutt before facing his final task in becoming a true Jedi – facing his father, Darth Vader, in battle. Luke prevailed when he refused to kill his father, balance was returned to the Force, and the galaxy was free from evil.

STATISTICS

SPECIES:	Human
HOMEWORLD:	Tatooine
HEIGHT:	1.72m
STRENGTH:	**9**
INTELLIGENCE:	**10**
SPECIAL ABILITIES:	**10** The Force
WEAPONRY:	**8** Lightsaber, blaster pistol
VEHICLE:	X-wing, snowspeeder, T-16 Skyhopper
BATTLE SKILLS:	**10** Lightsaber, The Force
ALLEGIANCE:	Rebel Alliance
ALLIES:	Princess Leia, Han Solo, R2-D2
ENEMIES:	Darth Vader, wampa, rancor

MAX REBO

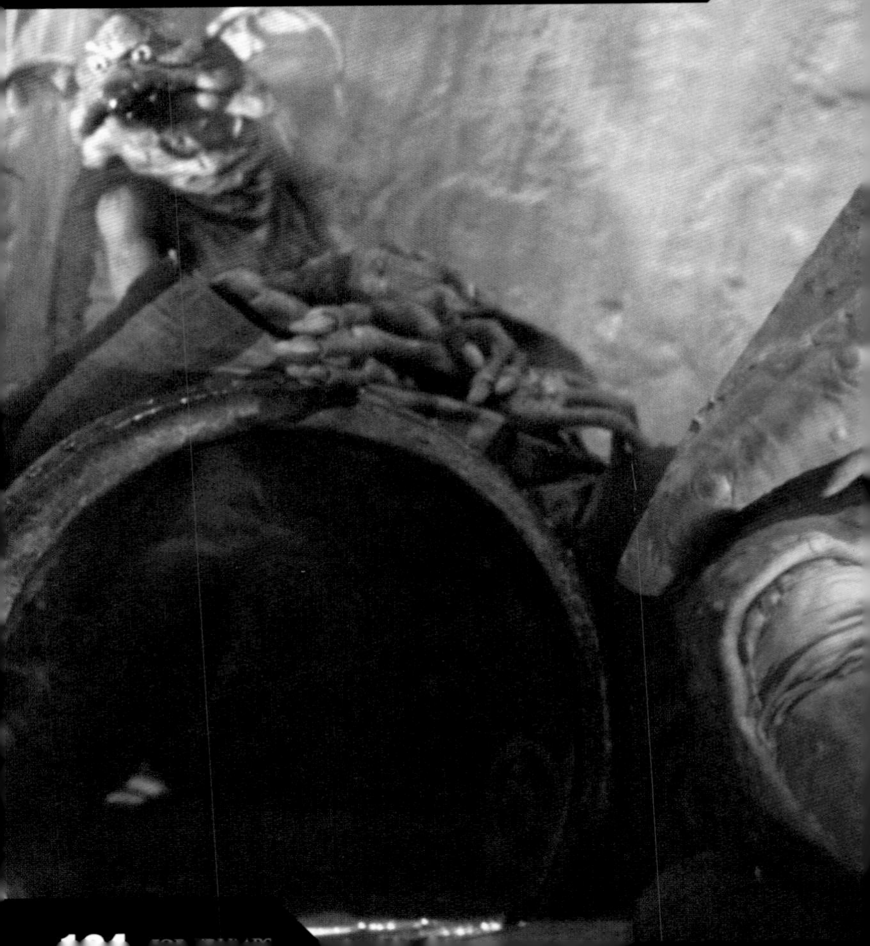

MAX REBO

Max Rebo was a blue-skinned Ortolan and quite the skilled musician. Although very talented, Rebo lacked any sort of business sense, often trading his services for food. Even though he thought more of his stomach than his accounts, Rebo managed to establish a reputation in the galaxy and a loyal band to play with him.

Jabba liked to be entertained almost as much as he liked ill-gotten wealth. He hired Max Rebo and his aptly named Max Rebo Band to play upbeat tunes in his throne room, allowing them to sign a lifetime contract as his court musicians. Much to the delight of the Hutt and his guests, Rebo kept a constant flow of hits coming from his Red Ball Jett keyboard, up to the fateful trip the Hutt and his entourage took to the Pit of Carkoon.

STATISTICS

SPECIES:	Ortolan
HOMEWORLD:	Orto
HEIGHT:	1.4m
STRENGTH:	**4**
INTELLIGENCE:	**6**
SPECIAL ABILITIES:	**7** Musician
WEAPONRY:	None
VEHICLE:	None
BATTLE SKILLS:	None
ALLEGIANCE:	Other / Neutral
ALLIES:	Sy Snootles, Jabba the Hutt
ENEMIES:	Unknown

During the final days of the Old Republic, Mon Mothma's voice was ne of the strongest among a group of oyalist Senators who called for an end o the dictatorship Palpatine had forged uring his tumultuous time as Chancellor. Vhen Palpatine declared himself mperor and ushered in the First Galactic mpire, Mothma had taken all she could tand. She and other Senators secretly nd formally established the Rebel lliance, an underground network whose ole purpose was to restore justice to the alaxy. She penned the "Declaration of ebellion," a moving piece that accused e Emperor of war crimes and drew opeful galactic citizens to the Rebel ause, and spent the next several years n the run from the Empire.

As Supreme Commander of the Rebel lliance, Mothma oversaw many battles, one as important as the final epic fight at took place above and on the forest oon of Endor. Mothma, along with dmiral Ackbar and General Crix Madine, utlined the plan of attack that would pple the Emperor and his minions nce and for all, and restore peace to war-torn galaxy.

STATISTICS

SPECIES:	Human
HOMEWORLD:	Chandrila
HEIGHT:	1.5m
STRENGTH:	**6**
INTELLIGENCE:	**10**
SPECIAL ABILITIES:	**10** Leadership
WEAPONRY:	Unknown
VEHICLE:	Unknown
BATTLE SKILLS:	**10** Battle plan analysis, leadership
ALLEGIANCE:	Rebel Alliance
ALLIES:	Admiral Ackbar, General Dodonna, Princess Leia
ENEMIES:	The Empire

OBI-WAN KENOBI

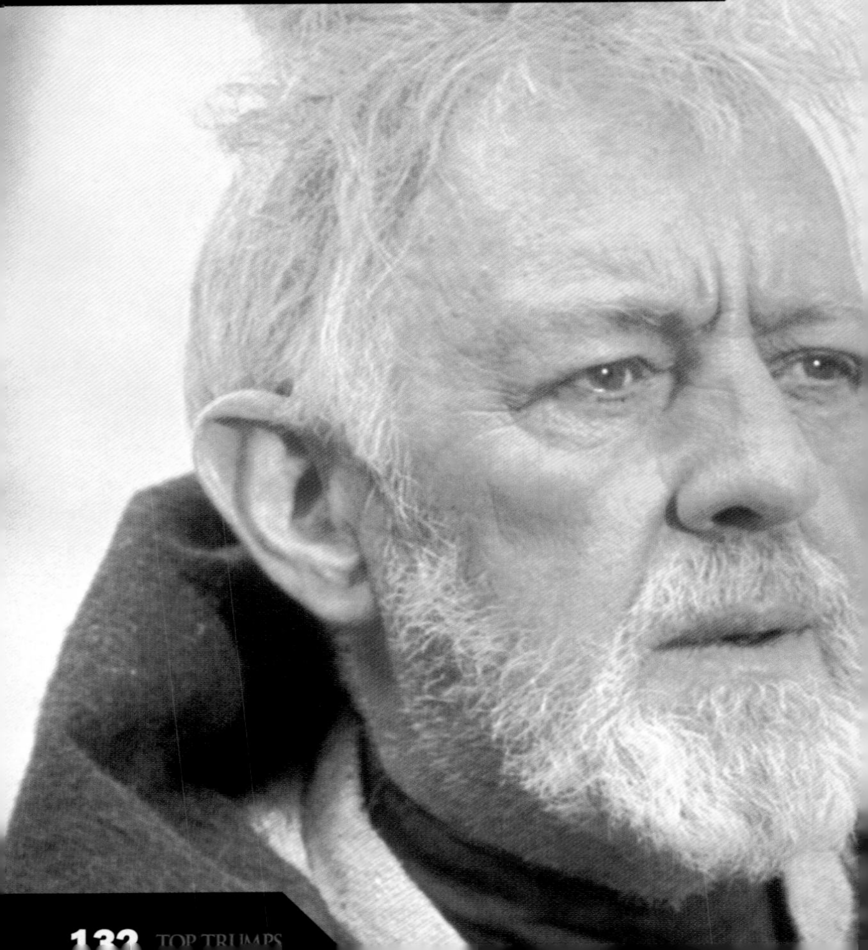

Obi-Wan Kenobi was a legendary Jedi Master during the time of the old Republic and a General in the Clone Wars. After his former Padawan Anakin Skywalker turned to the dark side and took the name Darth Vader, the two fought an epic battle that left Anakin scarred and dying. Obi-Wan took one of Padmé Amidala's newborn twins into hiding on the desert planet Tatooine. Delivering the newborn Luke Skywalker into the hands of the child's uncle Owen, Obi-Wan went into seclusion, waiting for the day that Luke would come to claim his destiny.

When that day came, Obi-Wan promised to train the boy to become a Jedi Knight. The two were en route to deliver R2-D2 and plans to the Death Star to Alderaan when they realized the planet had been destroyed. On board the Death Star after their ship was captured, Obi-Wan deactivated the tractor beam that was holding the ship prisoner and then came face-to-face with his former Padawan. The two fought for a second time, Darth Vader striking Obi-Wan down. His physical being now one with the Force, Obi-Wan was more powerful than ever before, and continued to guide Luke Skywalker on his path to becoming a Jedi Knight.

STATISTICS

SPECIES:	Human
HOMEWORLD:	Unknown
HEIGHT:	1.79m
STRENGTH:	**9**
INTELLIGENCE:	**10**
SPECIAL ABILITIES:	**10** Jedi Mind Control, the Force
WEAPONRY:	**10** Lightsaber
VEHICLE:	Unknown
BATTLE SKILLS:	**10** Lightsaber, hand-to-hand, military leadership, Jedi training
ALLEGIANCE:	Rebel Alliance
ALLIES:	Luke Skywalker, Han Solo, R2-D2, Yoda
ENEMIES:	Darth Vader

OWEN LARS

Owen Lars had toiled on his family's moisture farm from a young age, taking great pride in the discipline and hard work it took to maintain a successful homestead. His father, Cliegg Lars, had been a moisture farmer as well, and Owen stayed out on his family's farm along with his wife, Beru. With them lived their hard-working but impatient nephew Luke, a boy who longed for adventure.

Owen loved Luke and wanted to keep him safe from the truth that had brought him to Tatooine. Luke was anxious, asking to leave the farm and join the academy his friends attended. Owen relented, telling the boy he could go to the academy after one final season working on their farm.

Around the same time, Lars had purchased two droids from some passing Jawas, and unbeknownst to him, the droids were carrying information important to the Rebellion and the Empire. After R2-D2 escaped the Lars homestead, and Luke and C-3PO went to capture him, stormtroopers attacked the hapless farmer and his wife, laying waste to the Lars family home.

STATISTICS

SPECIES:	Human
HOMEWORLD:	Ator, Tatooine
HEIGHT:	1.78m
STRENGTH:	**6**
INTELLIGENCE:	**7**
SPECIAL ABILITIES:	**6** moisture farming
WEAPONRY:	Unknown
VEHICLE:	V-35 landspeeder, Zephyr-G swoop bike
BATTLE SKILLS:	Unknown
ALLEGIANCE:	Other / Neutral
ALLIES:	Luke Skywalker, Beru Lars
ENEMIES:	Tusken Raiders, stormtroopers

This aggressive Aqualish hails from the watery planet Ando. Aqualish are legendarily bad-tempered, and Ponda Baba does his best to maintain that reputation. He does not hesitate to announce his disapproval of fellow beings. If he doesn't like you, you are going to know about it.

Ponda Baba was Dr. Evazan's partner in crime after rescuing the psycho in the Corellian system. Ponda Baba was planning to turn the doctor in for the bounty, but realized that the two made a handy crime team. Together, they did many underhanded jobs for Jabba the Hutt, and often needed to travel to Tatooine. There, in a dark, crowded Mos Eisley cantina, the Aqualish grunted his dissatisfaction with Luke Skywalker, the result of which led to his arm being sliced off by Obi-Wan Kenobi's lightsaber.

STATISTICS

SPECIES:	Aqualish
HOMEWORLD:	Ando
HEIGHT:	1.85m
STRENGTH:	**7**
INTELLIGENCE:	**6**
SPECIAL ABILITIES:	**7** Bad temper
WEAPONRY:	**6** Blaster pistol
VEHICLE:	Unknown
BATTLE SKILLS:	**7** Rage
ALLEGIANCE:	Criminal
ALLIES:	Doctor Evazan, Jabba the Hutt
ENEMIES:	Luke Skywalker, Obi-Wan Kenobi

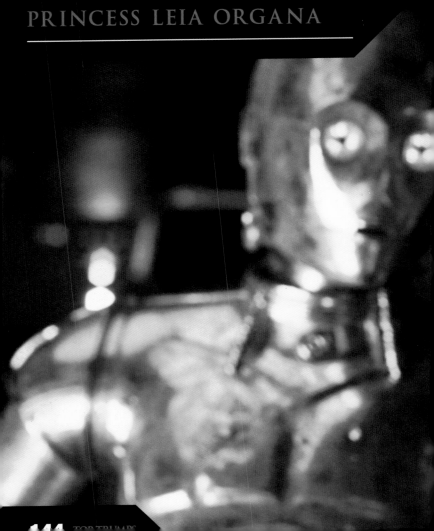

PRINCESS LEIA ORGANA

Princess Leia is the daughter of Anakin Skywalker and Senator Padmé Amidala. In order to protect her from Skywalker, who had turned to the dark side of the Force, she was separated at birth from her twin brother, Luke, and hidden from her father. She grew up happily unaware of her true parentage, and became a strong and respected galactic leader.

The adopted daughter of Bail Organa, Princess Leia Organa was the youngest member ever elected to the Imperial Senate. A dissenting voice against Emperor Palpatine's rule, Leia worked secretly as a member of the ever-growing Rebel Alliance. Carrying stolen plans to the Empire's ultimate weapon, the Death Star, Princess Leia was captured and taken prisoner. After being rescued, Leia oversaw the destruction of the Death Star. She continued to be a powerful and integral leader in the Rebellion, taking part in all major battles, including the final destruction of the Empire at Endor.

STATISTICS

SPECIES:	Human
HOMEWORLD:	Alderaan
HEIGHT:	1.5m
STRENGTH:	**6**
INTELLIGENCE:	**9**
SPECIAL ABILITIES:	**6** The Force
WEAPONRY:	**7** Blaster pistol
VEHICLE:	*Tantive IV*
BATTLE SKILLS:	**7** Blaster
ALLEGIANCE:	Rebel Alliance
ALLIES:	Luke Skywalker, Han Solo
ENEMIES:	Darth Vader, Jabba the Hutt

This R2-series astromech droid was designed by Industrial Automaton as a maintenance droid and mechanized starfighter companion, but has exceeded its programming countless times, proving itself to be one of the true heroes of the Rebellion.

Aboard the *Tantive IV*, Princess Leia stored the stolen plans to the Death Star in R2-D2 and gave the feisty droid an important mission – blast down to Tatooine's surface and find Jedi Master Obi-Wan Kenobi. Defying all odds, the little droid traversed the dangerous desert along with his companion, C-3PO, and accomplished his mission, ultimately delivering the plans to the Rebel base on Yavin 4 and then assisting Luke Skywalker as he destroyed the Death Star. R2 also accompanied Luke Skywalker on his mission to Dagobah, repaired the hyperdrive on the *Millennium Falcon* allowing Princess Leia to escape the clutches of Darth Vader at Cloud City, and helped rescue Han Solo from the clutches of Jabba the Hutt – all before his journey to Endor where he helped the Rebel Alliance defeat the Empire.

STATISTICS

DROID:	Industrial Automaton R2-series astromech
HOMEWORLD:	Naboo
HEIGHT:	0.96m
STRENGTH:	**4**
INTELLIGENCE:	**8**
SPECIAL ABILITIES:	**6** Flight, computer communication, mechanic skills
WEAPONRY:	**7** Arc welder, buzz saw
VEHICLE:	X-wing
BATTLE SKILLS:	**5** Assertiveness
ALLEGIANCE:	Rebel Alliance
ALLIES:	Luke Skywalker, Princess Leia, C-3PO, Obi-Wan Kenobi
ENEMIES:	Salacious Crumb, Jawas

RANCOR

Jabba the Hutt's palace was full of many unknown terrors, but none was so horrifying as that which lurked beneath the dais of his throne room. With a command, the evil Jabba could release a trap door that would send unwanted guests hurtling into the cavern below and straight into the clutches of a waiting beast. As Jabba and his entourage looked on, the degenerate spectacle took place.

The rancor is an enormous, carnivorous, reptilian beast with unusually long arms ending in huge, razor-sharp claws, its hulking, muscular body covered in thick blaster-resistant skin and supported by two stumpy legs. The main feature of its terrifying face is its fang-filled, drooling mouth that can engulf a hapless victim in one bite.

Jabba's rancor met its match in Jedi knight Luke Skywalker, however. When Luke was dropped into the rancor pit, he outsmarted the beast, first by propping its mouth open with a bone, and then by pinning it under a heavy, spiked gate.

STATISTICS

SPECIES:	Rancor
HOMEWORLD:	Unknown (possibly Dathomir)
HEIGHT:	5–10m
STRENGTH:	**8**
INTELLIGENCE:	**4**
SPECIAL ABILITIES:	None
WEAPONRY:	**7** Fangs, Claws
VEHICLE:	None
BATTLE SKILLS:	**6** Frenzied attack
ALLEGIANCE:	Other / Neutral
ALLIES:	Jabba the Hutt
ENEMIES:	Luke Skywalker

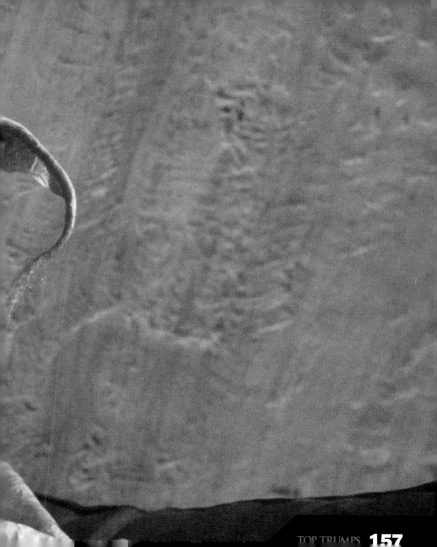

SALACIOUS CRUMB

This beaked, beady-eyed Kowakian monkey-lizard achieved his status as Jabba the Hutt's court jester by a silly twist of fate. Mantilorrian rat catchers aboard the Kwenn Space Station had failed repeatedly to catch the hideous vermin. He finally escaped the station by sneaking aboard Jabba's visiting ship. Jabba almost ate the cackling creature, but decided to keep Salacious as a pet after watching Bib Fortuna and Bidlo Kwerve bungle their attempts to catch the mischievous creature.

In Jabba's palace, Crumb sat on the throne and insulted visitors and prisoners by emitting a piercing, annoying cackle. He was particularly rude to C-3PO, who had recently been appointed Jabba's translator droid, by plucking out the droid's photoreceptor during Luke Skywalker's heroic rescue of Han Solo and friends. R2-D2 shocked the nasty creature, however, sending him flying away from C-3PO. Salacious Crumb's last known action was a rude remark aimed at the astromech droid while dangling from a rafter on Jabba's sail barge.

STATISTICS

SPECIES:	Kowakian monkey-lizard
HOMEWORLD:	Kowak
HEIGHT:	0.7m
STRENGTH:	**2**
INTELLIGENCE:	**4**
SPECIAL ABILITIES:	None
WEAPONRY:	None
VEHICLE:	None
BATTLE SKILLS:	None
ALLEGIANCE:	Bounty Hunter / Criminal
ALLIES:	Jabba the Hutt
ENEMIES:	C-3PO, R2-D2

STORMTROOPERS

Encased in white armour, these soldiers of the Empire are its most visible presence, appearing in almost every port on almost every populated planet in the galaxy. Their numbers are countless, and they act both as ground police and as part of the Imperial Starfleet. Totally loyal to Emperor Palpatine, stormtroopers serve without question and with little regard to their own safety.

Stormtroopers have comlinks in their helmets in order to communicate with one another more effectively. Officers have special shoulder pauldrons. Different environments call for special abilities, so certain stormtroopers are trained to operate in snow, desert or forest terrain. These troopers have modified armor created specifically for their assignments.

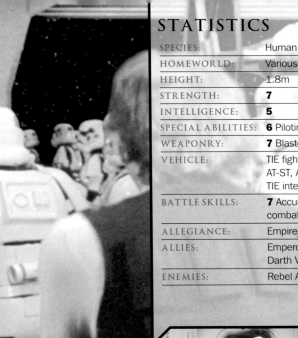

STATISTICS

SPECIES:	Human
HOMEWORLD:	Various
HEIGHT:	1.8m
STRENGTH:	**7**
INTELLIGENCE:	**5**
SPECIAL ABILITIES:	**6** Piloting
WEAPONRY:	**7** Blaster rifle
VEHICLE:	TIE fighter, speeder bike, AT-ST, AT-AT, TIE bomber, TIE interceptor
BATTLE SKILLS:	**7** Accuracy, combat training
ALLEGIANCE:	Empire
ALLIES:	Emperor Palpatine, Darth Vader
ENEMIES:	Rebel Alliance

TUSKEN RAIDERS

Covered from head to foot in distinctive tribal wrappings, Tusken Raiders, or Sand People as they're also known, traverse the Dundland Wastes of Tatooine in packs, attacking fiercely and mercilessly wayward travellers and Jawa colonies. Males, females and children each wear unique costumes, and a Tusken Raider who happens to show his skin, even by accident, is banished from the tribe.

Tusken Raiders have domesticated Tatooine banthas as mounts and form symbiotic relationships with their partner animals as part of a rite of passage from youth to adulthood.

A group of Tusken Raiders spotted Luke Skywalker and C-3PO as they raced through the desert in search of a determined R2-D2. When the farm boy and protocol droid finally caught up with the astromech, R2 alerted them to the Raiders' presence, but it was too late – the Tusken Raiders staged an attack and knocked Luke unconscious. Jedi Master Obi-Wan Kenobi showed up just in time and scared the skittish Tusken Raiders away with a piercing cry imitating a krayt dragon.

STATISTICS

SPECIES:	Tusken Raider (species unknown)
HOMEWORLD:	Tatooine
HEIGHT:	1.8m
STRENGTH:	**8**
INTELLIGENCE:	**4**
SPECIAL ABILITIES:	None
WEAPONRY:	**6** Gaderffii, projectile rifle
VEHICLE:	None
BATTLE SKILLS:	**6** Frenzied attack
ALLEGIANCE:	Other / Neutral
ALLIES:	None
ENEMIES:	Krayt dragon and everyone

WAMPA

The ice planet Hoth is dangerous for many reasons, not the least of which is its permanent winter, with nighttime temperatures too cold for even native species to survive. Far more perilous than the weather, however, is the dreaded wampa ice creature, an enormous mammal covered in camouflaging white fur. Its razor-sharp claws make it a deadly hunter, feeding mostly on hapless tauntauns. This native species digs caves into the permanent ice on the planet's surface, dragging its prey back to the shelter and suspending the carcasses from the cave ceiling until ready to eat.

When the Rebel Alliance chose Hoth as its new hidden base after the Battle of Yavin, a wampa attacked Commander Luke Skywalker as he was checking a meteor sighting. Both he and his sturdy tauntaun fell victim to the beast, but Luke managed to regain consciousness long enough to summon his lightsaber, free himself from his icy prison, and injure the creature before it could attack him.

STATISTICS

SPECIES:	Wampa
HOMEWORLD:	Hoth
HEIGHT:	3m
STRENGTH:	**9**
INTELLIGENCE:	**3**
SPECIAL ABILITIES:	**6** Rage, camouflage
WEAPONRY:	**7** Razor-sharp claws, teeth
VEHICLE:	None
BATTLE SKILLS:	**8**
ALLEGIANCE:	Other / Neutral
ALLIES:	None
ENEMIES:	None

WEDGE ANTILLES

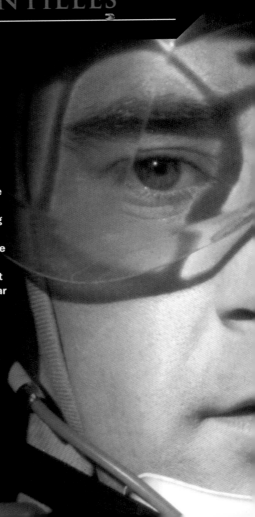

WEDGE ANTILLES

Wedge Antilles, leader of the elite group of rebel pilots known as Rogue Squadron, was a true hero in the fight against the Empire.

Wedge was with the rebellion from the beginning. After his parents were killed, Antilles bought a freighter and smuggled weapons to the rebellion. He then joined the Alliance full-time as an X-wing pilot. He fought alongside Luke Skywalker in some of the most famous battles against the Empire, including the fight against the original Death Star and the defence against the Empire's ground assault on Hoth. In the Battle of Endor, Antilles led the final assault against the Death Star, flying directly into its core, helping Lando Calrissian destroy it.

STATISTICS

SPECIES:	Human
HOMEWORLD:	Corellia
HEIGHT:	1.7m
STRENGTH:	**7**
INTELLIGENCE:	**7**
SPECIAL ABILITIES:	**8** Leadership
WEAPONRY:	**6** Blaster pistol
VEHICLE:	X-wing
BATTLE SKILLS:	**9** Piloting, Accuracy
ALLEGIANCE:	Rebel Alliance
ALLIES:	Luke Skywalker
ENEMIES:	The Empire

WICKET W. WARRICK

This inquisitive, adventurous Ewok was the great grandson of legendary Ewok warrior Erpham Warrick. He grew up in Bright Tree Village on the forest moon of Endor along with his brothers, Weechee and Widdle, and his baby sister, Winda. His curious nature often led him on treks through the forests that surrounded his home and led to his becoming a scout for the Ewok tribe.

On one such scouting mission, Wicket stumbled upon an unconscious Princess Leia, who had been thrown from her speeder bike during a chase. He prodded her awake with his spear, and although wary of her at first, quickly became friends with the lovely Princess. He led her to his village. There, she and the other Rebels soon gained acceptance within the Ewok tribe. Wicket accompanied the Rebels on a scouting mission to the back entrance to the Empire's shield generator bunker and, when he discovered the Rebels had been led into a trap, sought the help of the entire Ewok tribe. With Wicket's assistance, the Rebellion defeated the Empire both on the surface of Endor and in the space above its verdant surface.

STATISTICS

SPECIES:	Ewok
HOMEWORLD:	Endor
HEIGHT:	0.8m
STRENGTH:	**4**
INTELLIGENCE:	**7**
SPECIAL ABILITIES:	**8** Scouting
WEAPONRY:	**4** Spear
VEHICLE:	None
BATTLE SKILLS:	**5** Surprise attack
ALLEGIANCE:	Rebel Alliance
ALLIES:	Princess Leia, C-3PO, R2-D2
ENEMIES:	Stormtroopers

YODA

Little did Luke know as he was arguing with the diminutive green figure in the murky swamps of Dagobah that he was, in fact, talking to one of the wisest, most powerful Jedi Masters in the history of the Republic.

Yoda had trained Jedi for 800 years and been a leader in the Clone Wars before he crossed paths with Luke. Yoda's final student had travelled to the jungle world after a vision of Obi-Wan Kenobi instructed him to seek out Yoda and complete his Jedi training. Through the vines, bogs and swamps, Yoda taught Luke to control his emotions and feel the Force. Although Luke left in the middle of his training after a horrible vision of his friends in peril, Yoda's Jedi teachings prevailed and helped Luke resist the dark side. When Luke returned to Dagobah, he found an ailing Yoda who revealed that Darth Vader was Luke's father and that Luke had a twin sister. Yoda gave Luke one final test to become a Jedi and then became one with the Force.

STATISTICS

SPECIES:	Unknown
HOMEWORLD:	Unknown
HEIGHT:	0.66m
STRENGTH:	**10**
INTELLIGENCE:	**10**
SPECIAL ABILITIES:	**10** Levitation, the Force, mind reading, seeing the future
WEAPONRY:	**10** Lightsaber
VEHICLE:	None
BATTLE SKILLS:	**10** Lightsaber
ALLEGIANCE:	Rebel Alliance
ALLIES:	Luke Skywalker, Obi-Wan Kenobi
ENEMIES:	Darth Vader, Emperor Palpatine

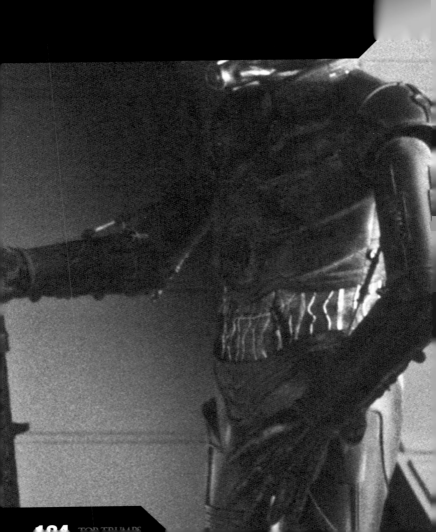

ZUCKUSS

Carrying on the ancient hunting traditions of his people, Zuckuss is known as a Gand Findsman. This insectoid alien uses mystical rituals and visions to help him ensnare his targets. Zuckuss is a rare subspecies of Gand called a "breather." Most Gand receive all vital nutrients through their food, but Zuckuss and others in his subspecies inhale the misty, ammonia-rich atmosphere on their homeworld. Zuckuss needs to wear a breathing mask and carry tanks filled with ammonia in order to survive off the surface of his planet.

When Darth Vader, fed up with the Empire's inability to capture Han Solo and the *Millennium Falcon*, assembled some of the galaxy's most feared bounty hunters, Zuckuss was there, prepared to use his uncanny abilities to track and capture the Corellian Rebel hero and his companions.

STATISTICS

SPECIES:	Gand
HOMEWORLD:	Gand
HEIGHT:	1.5m
STRENGTH:	**6**
INTELLIGENCE:	**8**
SPECIAL ABILITIES:	**8** Gand Findsman rituals, visions
WEAPONRY:	**9** Blaster pistol, stun grenades, Merr-Sonn Munitions GRS-1 snare rifle
VEHICLE:	*Mist Hunter*
BATTLE SKILLS:	**6**
ALLEGIANCE:	Bounty hunter / Criminal
ALLIES:	4-LOM
ENEMIES:	Boba Fett

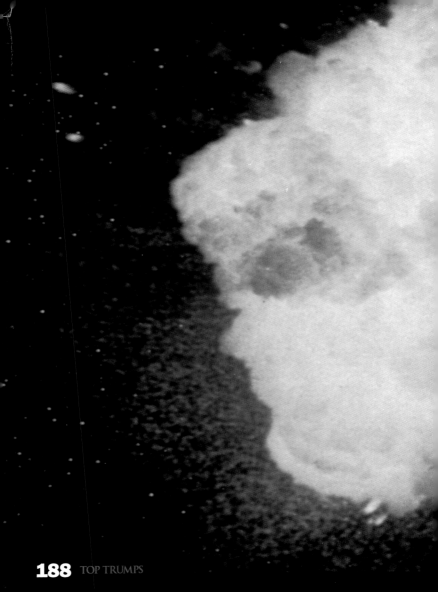